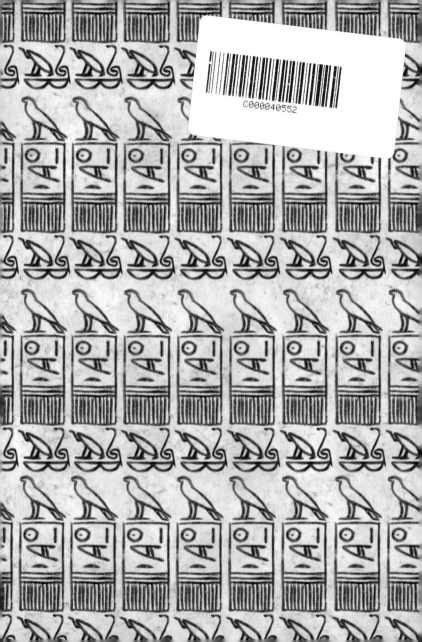

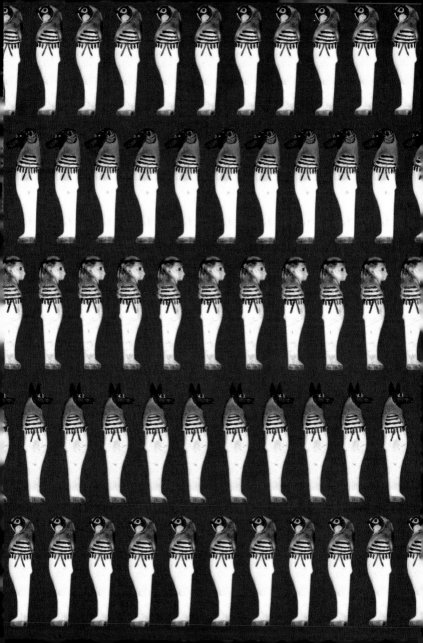

The British Museum

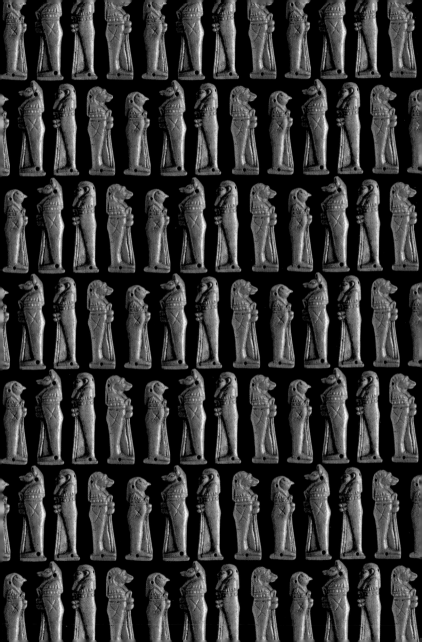

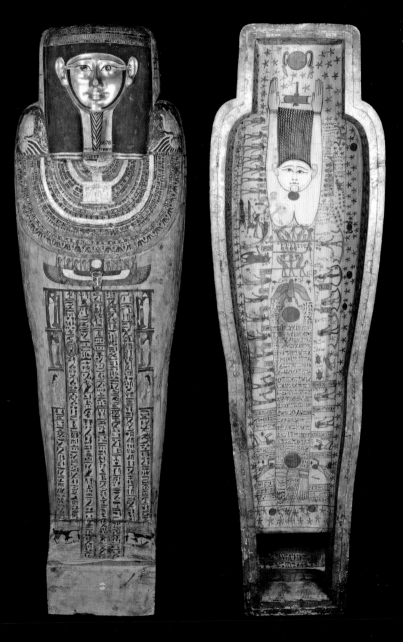

The British
Museum

Inner coffin of the priest Hornedjitef, Early Ptolemaic Period,
3rd century BC, Thebes, Egypt
British Museum Department of Ancient Egypt and Sudan
© The Trustees of the British Museum

The British Museum

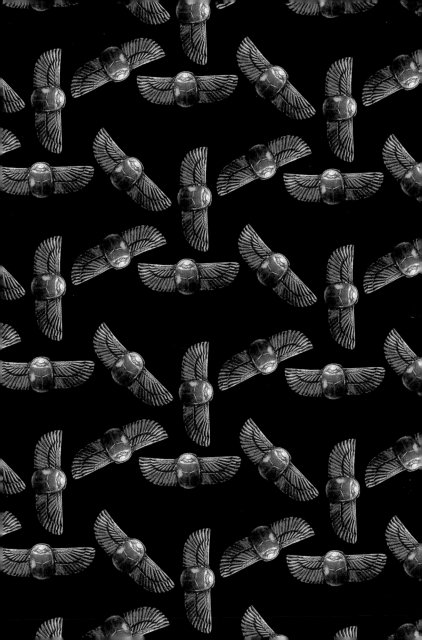

The British Museum

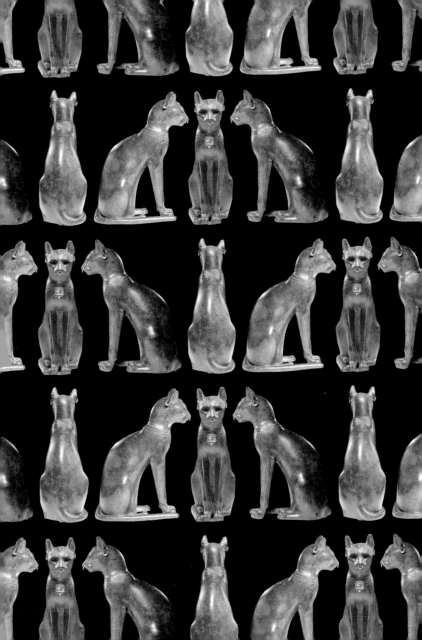

'The Gayer-Anderson Cat', bronze figure of a seated cat,
Late Period, c.664-332BC, possibly from Saqqara, Egypt
British Museum Department of Ancient Egypt and Sudan

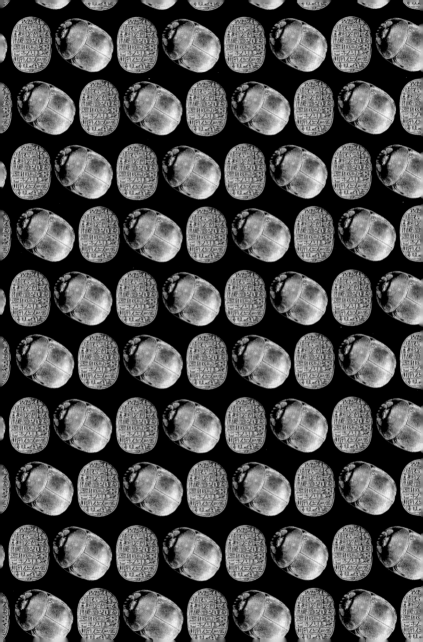

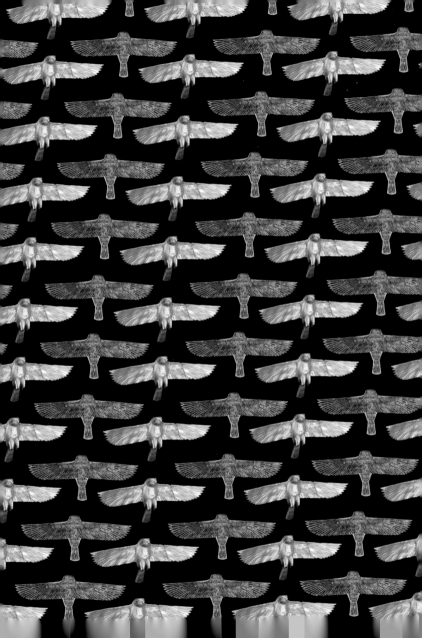

The British Museum

Gold pectoral representing a falcon, Late or Ptolemaic Period,
600–200BC, Egypt
British Museum Department of Ancient Egypt and Sudan
© The Trustees of the British Museum

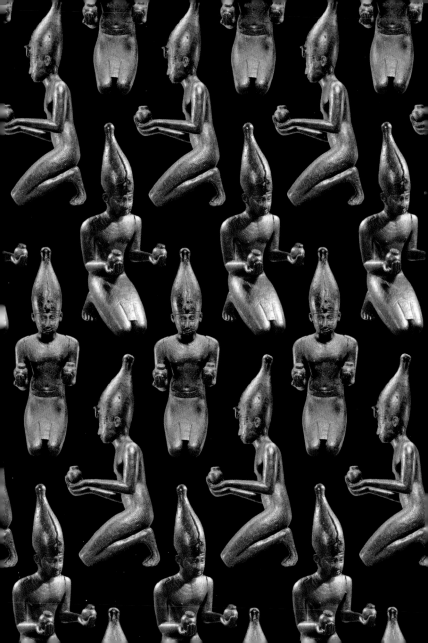

The British
Museum

Bronze kneeling figure of King Pimay, 22nd Dynasty,
c.773-767BC, Egypt
British Museum Department of Ancient Egypt and Sudan
© The Trustees of the British Museum

Book of the Dead papyrus of the Chantress of Amun, Anhai,
20th Dynasty, c.1100BC; probably Thebes, Egypt
British Museum Department of Ancient Egypt and Sudan
© The Trustees of the British Museum

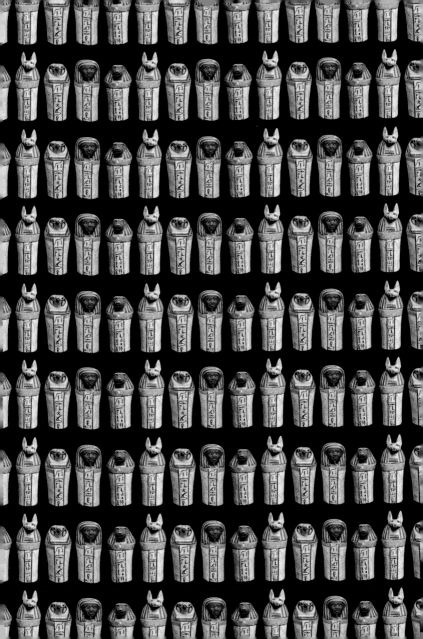

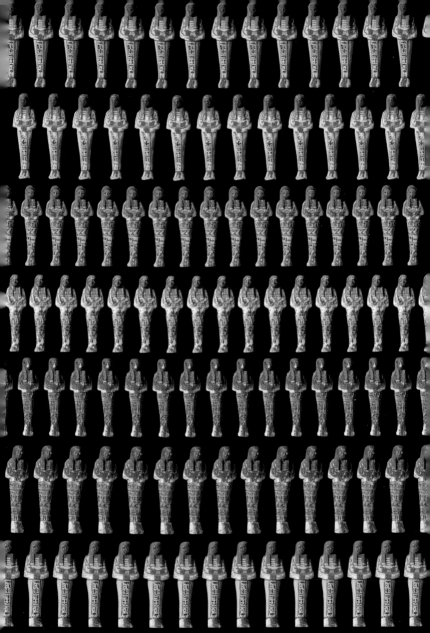

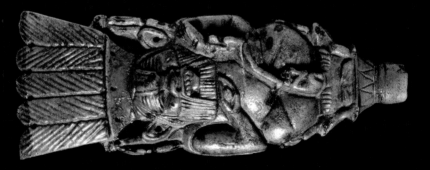

The British Museum